This book belongs to

_____

This book is dedicated to my children - Mikey, Kobe, and Jojo.

978-1-63731-226-1 Printed and bound in the USA. MiniMovers.tv

Michael Jordan

By Mary Nhin

Pictures By
Yuliia Zolotova

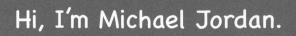
Hi, I'm Michael Jordan.

I grew up playing many different sports including baseball and basketball. I practiced a lot with my brothers, but especially, my older brother, Larry.

Larry was stronger and taller which gave me great competition. Every evening, we played baseball using our barbecue pit as the backstop and a tennis ball as the baseball.

Competing with Larry fueled my competitive spirit. I wanted to be just as good as my brother.

When I was in high school, I tried out for the school's basketball varsity team, but I failed to make the team. At 5'11", I was told that I was too short.

This rejection just made me even more determined to play. My height wasn't something that I could control, but I could control my skills.

That's when I focused on practicing to improve.

I joined the junior varsity team and practiced as much as I could.

I wanted to prove that I deserved a spot on the varsity team, so I worked hard in the junior tournaments, becoming the team's star player of the year.

Some people want it to happen, some wish it would happen, others make it happen.

I worked hard, but I also grew four inches. And when I tried out for the varsity team the following school year, I was ready.

I played for the varsity team and was offered college basketball scholarships. After much debating, I decided to play at North Carolina.

It was during college that people began to notice my talent. We reached the NCAA Championship, and I helped my team win with a jump shot.

Soon, I was drafted in the third round of the NBA draft. I was going to play professional basketball and do what I love. I was so happy!

The Chicago Bulls choose Michael Jordan.

NBA DRAFT 84

My passion and determination to win showed every time I played. I became a fan favorite, even though the game didn't always go my way.

My leaping ability, demonstrated by performing slam dunks from the free throw line, earned me the nicknames "Air Jordan" and "His Airness."

Then finally, in 1991, my dream came true. Our team, the Chicago Bulls, won first place! And, I took home the NBA Finals MVP Award for the first time in my career.

We went on to win the next two years to complete our first three-peat. Then, we did it again in 1995-1998 for a second three-peat.

And that is why I succeed.

Timeline

1984 - Air Jordans debut

1988 – MJ wins the NBA Defensive Player of
the Year Award

1991 – MJ and the Chicago Bulls win the NBA Championship
for the first time. MJ wins the NBA Finals Most Valuable
Player Award

1992 - MJ and the Chicago Bulls win the NBA
championship for the second time

1993 - MJ and Chicago Bulls complete a three-peat

1996 - MJ plays himself in Space Jam

1998 - MJ and Chicago Bulls complete a second three-peat

2015 – MJ is inducted into the FIBA Basketball
Hall of Fame

minimovers.tv

 @marynhin   @GrowGrit
#minimoversandshakers

 Mary Nhin   Ninja Life Hacks

 Ninja Life Hacks

Printed in the USA
CPSIA information can be obtained
at www.ICGtesting.com
LVHW071649301023
762357LV00044B/167

9781637312285